THE U.S.-REPUBLIC OF KOREA-JAPAN TRILATERAL RELATIONSHIP: PROMOTING MUTUAL INTERESTS IN ASIA

HEARING

BEFORE THE

SUBCOMMITTEE ON ASIA AND THE PACIFIC

OF THE

COMMITTEE ON FOREIGN AFFAIRS
HOUSE OF REPRESENTATIVES

ONE HUNDRED FOURTEENTH CONGRESS

SECOND SESSION

SEPTEMBER 27, 2016

Serial No. 114–233

Printed for the use of the Committee on Foreign Affairs

Available via the World Wide Web: http://www.foreignaffairs.house.gov/ or
http://www.gpo.gov/fdsys/

U.S. GOVERNMENT PUBLISHING OFFICE

21–674PDF   WASHINGTON : 2016

For sale by the Superintendent of Documents, U.S. Government Publishing Office
Internet: bookstore.gpo.gov   Phone: toll free (866) 512–1800; DC area (202) 512–1800
Fax: (202) 512–2104   Mail: Stop IDCC, Washington, DC 20402–0001

CONTENTS

THE U.S.-REPUBLIC OF KOREA-JAPAN TRILATERAL RELATIONSHIP: PROMOTING MUTUAL INTERESTS IN ASIA

TUESDAY, SEPTEMBER 27, 2016

House of Representatives,
Subcommittee on Asia and the Pacific,
Committee on Foreign Affairs,
Washington, DC.

The subcommittee met, pursuant to notice, at 2:50 p.m., in room 2172, Rayburn House Office Building, Hon. Matt Salmon (chairman of the subcommittee) presiding.

Mr. SALMON. The subcommittee will come to order.

Members present will be permitted to submit written statements to be included in the official hearing record.

Without objection, the hearing record will remain open for 5 calendar days to allow statements, questions, extraneous materials for this record subject to the length limitation in the rules.

When officials say that the United States is a Pacific power, they are not just making an empty talking point. Our country has deep and enduring interests in Asia Pacific, from business and trade deals with the world's fastest growing economies to serious national security threats from both rogue States and great powers alike.

To conduct these important affairs, we have created a hub-and-spoke system of like-minded allies and partners throughout the region, a bloc of friends who can mutually reinforce each other's best interests.

The Republic of Korea and Japan are perhaps the United States' most constant and important partners within the system. Economically developed and militarily capable, these two nations share our democratic values and national security interests, which drives strong bilateral relations. Going forward, I believe these shared positions will ensure that these alliances coalesce into a comprehensive trilateral relationship.

As we all know, earlier this month, North Korea launched multiple missiles toward Japan and detonated its largest nuclear device to date. Our current sanctions-based approach to deterrence has little to no effect on North Korea's nuclear program, and we need to work closely with our allies to meet this challenge.

Following North Korea's most recent provocations, Secretary Kerry met with his counterparts, Foreign Minister Kishida of Japan and Foreign Minister Yun Byung-se of Korea. Deputy Sec-

FORMAT

retary Blinken has made great strides in promoting and facilitating a greater trilateral relationship as well. The increasing security threat posed by North Korea's rogue regime underscored yet again this trilateral relationship's importance.

U.S. foreign policy is subjected to the transitional period of elections and a change of administration over the coming months. It is imperative that the value of this trilateral cooperation is not neglected and that the positive trend of closer cooperation continues.

Korea and Japan have long endured legacy issues that have created domestic friction that hindered their relationship and limit their own bilateral cooperation. But over the last year, the world has witnessed Prime Minister Abe and President Park leading their countries in historic steps toward a closer and more productive relationship. I commend each of them for their courage to take those important strides, resulting in a positive influence on the strategic outlook of the region and demonstrating even more promise for the future. The past year has seen improved military diplomacy and intercommunications, including a new hotline between Defense Ministers and the first trilateral missile defense exercise with the U.S., and I hope there is more to come.

In late May, President Obama traveled to Hiroshima, where he met with survivors of the atomic explosion and made nuclear policy recommendations for the future. This summer, the Japanese First Lady Akie Abe visited Pearl Harbor and paid her respects to those who died in the surprise attack that pulled our Nation into war with Japan. This type of diplomacy, quietly working to heal old wounds without getting hung up on explicit apologies, is commendable and can serve as a model to our close allies, the Republic of Korea and Japan.

Today's Asia poses innumerable challenges to those who believe in personal liberties, free markets, Democratic governance, and peaceful dispute resolution. We face nuclear belligerence, territorial aggression, and serious competition from an ideology that supposes a less free society and economy brings greater success. In each of these realms, our national interests are aligned with those of the Republic of Korea and of Japan, not through any coercion or persuasion, but because we fundamentally agree.

By encouraging these two allies to cooperate more closely in the context of our trilateral relationship, we will be able to address mutual challenges in a more united and robust manner. To this end, I hope that we will continue to see closer cooperation between the Republic of Korea and Japan, including meaningful dialogue between national leaders and increasing military exercises. I also strongly urge our allies to implement the terms of the agreement on comfort women quickly and to the satisfaction of both sides.

And finally, I hope that the parties involved work to promote better relations among Japan and Korea's populations at large. We are grateful that Assistant Secretary Russel joins us here today, and I look forward to hearing his expertise firsthand and his suggestions on strengthening this critical trilateral relationship.

And with that, I recognize Mr. Sherman before we hear from our witness.

Mr. SHERMAN. Thank you, Mr. Chairman, for holding these hearings.

Our relationship with the Republic of Korea and with Japan are the bedrock of U.S. economic and military interests in the East Asia-Pacific region. And we have intense person-to-person ties, since 1 percent of all Americans are either Japanese Americans or Korean Americans, Japanese American population of our country being 1.3 million, Korean American population being 1.7. And I am proud to say that, by far, the largest contingent of Japanese and Korean Americans are in California.

As to North Korea, this year marks the 10th anniversary of the North Korean nuclear tests. We have seen expansions in their missile program. The easiest thing for the State Department and the rest of the foreign policy bureaucracy to do is to advocate that we continue the same policies, that we embark on new show of force, that we get the predictable reaction from South Korea and Japan. Of course, over the last 10 years, this has not been accompanied by a change in North Korean policy, unless the expansion of their nuclear arsenal and the expansion of their missile capabilities constitutes a change.

What is even more worrying is that now with 12 nuclear weapons and the ability to produce additional fissile material, North Korea may believe that it has enough nuclear weapons to defend itself from us and is free to sell a surplus. We see that North Korea has cooperated with Iran on missile technology, but even more to the point was that over a decade ago, North Korea transferred to Syria or Syria and Iran, in effect, a kit to build nuclear weapons. This was destroyed by Israel in eastern Syria in 2007. But now, North Korea is in a position, not just to transfer a kit on how someone else may create their own fissile material, but rather they are in a position to transfer the fissile material or to transfer a completed weapon.

We need Japan and North Korea to join us in increasing economic and diplomatic pressure on China, because without a change in China's behavior, we will not see a change in North Korea's behavior. While we have to respect our mutual security treaties, and especially the nonproliferation treaty, we do need to see a better balance in our relationship with Japan and South Korea, balance in defense spending and burden sharing and balance in trade.

As to defense spending, South Korea spends 2.6 percent of its GDP on its defense, even though it is on the frontline literally, with property in northern Seoul selling for less than southern Seoul simply because of how close it is to the frontline. Japan spends 1 percent of its GDP on military expenditures. Certainly, countries that close to the threat should be spending more than those who—than a country protected by the Atlantic and Pacific Ocean as part of its—as a percentage of its GDP.

As to trade, through July of this year, we are looking at a $40-billion trade deficit with Japan, $19-billion trade deficit with South Korea. And, of course, that deficit with South Korea is considerably higher since we adopted the KORUS Free Trade Agreement. Obviously, those trade deficits translate into job loss. Some economists would say 10,000 jobs for every $1 billion of trade deficit.

So I look forward to a policy that nudges the Japanese and South Koreans into a more balanced relationship with the United States on trade, more balance in terms of defense spending, and a balanced and coordinated effort to push Beijing into a policy that changes North Korean behavior.

And, with that, I yield back.

Mr. SALMON. Thank you.

We are joined today by Assistant Secretary Danny Russel of the Bureau of East Asian Affairs. And for the record, I am a big fan of his. I think he does a really great job, And we are grateful for your willingness to share your expertise with this committee, and I will turn the time over to you, Mr. Russel.

STATEMENT OF THE HONORABLE DANIEL R. RUSSEL, ASSISTANT SECRETARY, BUREAU OF EAST ASIAN AND PACIFIC AFFAIRS, U.S. DEPARTMENT OF STATE

Mr. RUSSEL. Thank you.

Chairman Salmon, Ranking Member Sherman, members of the subcommittee, thanks very much for holding this very timely hearing on the U.S.-Japan-Republic of Korea trilateral cooperation. Thank you also for your recognition of the diplomatic work that we are doing. And, most importantly, thank you for the strong support you provide to our Asia policy.

Our trilateral cooperation reflects the increasingly network nature of America's alliances and partnerships in the Asia Pacific under President Obama's rebalance. It is also worth mentioning our longstanding trilateral security dialogue with Australia and Japan and a separate process with India and Japan as examples of trilateral cooperation with important democratic partners in many areas where our interests align.

Mr. Chairman, as you pointed out, we are bound to Japan and Korea by treaties, by thriving economic relationships, shared values, common threats, and, as the President said in March after a trilateral leaders meeting here in Washington, by the enduring bonds between our people. And I am pleased to report that our trilateral cooperation has helped to foster improved ties between Japan and Korea. As you alluded to, their December 2015 agreement on comfort women marked a courageous step to promote healing and reconciliation. And this has paved the way for us to do much more together.

Our trilateral engagement overall has evolved into a global partnership, helping to maximize our ability to address the interconnected challenges of an interconnected world. For example, just last week, Vice President Biden held a trilateral meeting on his Cancer Moonshot Initiative in New York with the Japanese Ministers of Health and the Korean Minister of Health.

The President, Secretary Kerry, the Secretary of Defense, Deputy Secretary Blinken, have each held trilateral meetings with their Korean and Japanese counterparts this year on issues ranging from trade and climate change, cybersecurity, violent extremism. In fact, there is a trilateral women's empowerment forum meeting taking place in Washington today. We are strengthening our capacity in Asia and beyond by coordinating the assistance programs of the three countries. This is a good way to avoid the costs of intervening later after a crisis.

But countering the threat from North Korea's growing nuclear and missile program is our most important area of trilateral cooperation. Our three countries have increased military interoperability, a highly cost-effective force multiplier. We have increased our diplomatic and defense coordination through a variety of mechanisms, including an information sharing agreement.

At the Deputy Secretary level, Tony Blinken maintains a regular, in-depth trial log. We have instituted trilateral military exercises like Pacific Dragon, a missile warning exercise we just conducted this past June. And we hold chiefs of defense and other important coordination meetings. We move in lockstep to counter North Korea's proliferation activities, including outreach to all members of the United Nations to help them fully implement their obligations under Security Council resolutions.

And the net effect of this effort is we are disrupting the north's arms trade, we are deflagging their ships, we are cutting off their external revenues, such as that generated by overseas workers. We are using multilateral fora to obtain clear international condemnation of North Korea's dangerous actions.

So together, our three countries are imposing higher and higher costs on North Korea, not to bring Pyongyang to its knees, but to bring it to its senses. The pressure will mount until the north agrees to return to negotiations on denuclearization and comply with its international commitments. But, let me be clear, the door to a diplomatic solution remains open. North Korea can choose a better path as Iran, Cuba, Burma have done.

Lastly, Mr. Chairman, and importantly, we are standing up for universal values and the rule of law. And I am convinced that over the long term, the greatest force multiplier in foreign affairs is the support of a network of like-minded democracies. Our trilateral cooperation grows out of these shared interests and adherence to democratic principles.

Before I end, Mr. Chairman, allow me on behalf of the Department of State to please express our deep thanks to you personally for your dedication, for your contributions to American foreign policy in Asia, for your leadership as chair of this subcommittee. You have been a great leader and a great partner. Thank you very much.

[The prepared statement of Mr. Russel follows:]

Statement of
Daniel R. Russel
Assistant Secretary
Bureau of East Asian and Pacific Affairs
U.S. Department of State

Before the

House Foreign Affairs Committee
Subcommittee on Asia and the Pacific

September 27, 2016

Trilateral Cooperation Between the United States,
Japan, and the Republic of Korea

Chairman Salmon, Ranking Member Sherman, and Members of the Subcommittee: thank you for the opportunity to appear before you today to testify on the topic of trilateral cooperation among the United States, Japan, and the Republic of Korea. I would also like to thank the Committee for holding a hearing on this important topic. The ongoing threat posed by North Korea's unlawful nuclear and ballistic missile programs, as reflected in their latest nuclear test on September 9 and accelerating pace of launches this year, brings the importance of our trilateral cooperation into sharper focus.

U.S-Japan-ROK Cooperation

The Rebalance to the Asia-Pacific has been a centerpiece initiative of the Obama Administration, which has recognized that events and developments in that region over the coming decades will deeply influence our nation's security and prosperity. A fundamental objective of that strategy has been to revitalize our treaty alliances and to establish networks among them. One of the best examples of such networking is the increasingly strong trilateral relationship with two of our closest friends, Japan and the Republic of Korea.

Our three countries are bound by shared values and interests, and the common threats we face. Our alliances with both countries, embodied in the U.S. - Republic of Korea Mutual Defense Treaty and the U.S.-Japan Treaty of Mutual Cooperation and Security, are longstanding and unshakeable. The ties of trade and investment among our three economies, the world's first, third, and eleventh largest, are fundamental to our interconnected world and U.S. prosperity.

We share many of the same concerns and face the same threats in the region, including the one posed by a nuclear North Korea. But most importantly, the United States, the Republic of Korea, and Japan are bound by our agreement on the core principles and values that undergird the success of our countries – democracy, human rights, open markets, and the paramount importance of the rule of law. As three advanced democracies and market economies, it is natural that we cooperate on more than regional issues, harnessing the power of our governments, scientists, business leaders, and civil societies to make progress in tackling global problems.

The Shared Threat of North Korea

The United States, the Republic of Korea, and Japan together face the region's most acute threat – North Korea. On September 9, North Korea conducted its fifth nuclear test, the second this year. This test followed an unprecedented spate of ballistic missile launches, 22 so far this year. These provocations have become far too common and threaten the security of the United States and our allies. Mr. Chairman, as the House noted in H.Res.634, North Korea's ongoing nuclear and missile tests represent direct and egregious violations of United Nations Security Council Resolutions and make clear that North Korea has no regard for international norms and standards.

As President Obama said shortly after the September 9 nuclear test, the United States condemns North Korea's nuclear and missile tests in the strongest possible terms as a grave threat to regional security and to international peace and stability. The United States does not, and will not, accept North Korea as a nuclear weapons state. Shortly after North Korea's September 9 nuclear test, President Obama spoke with President Park of the Republic of Korea and Prime Minister Abe of Japan and agreed to work with UN Security Council members, our other Six-Party partners, and the broader international community to implement vigorously the existing measures imposed by previous resolutions, and to take additional significant steps, including new measures, to demonstrate to North Korea that there are consequences for its unlawful and dangerous actions. We are also considering possible trilateral measures with the ROK and Japan in response to North Korea's destabilizing actions. President Obama has restated the unshakeable U.S. commitment to defend the ROK and Japan against the North Korean threat and to provide extended deterrence, guaranteed by the full spectrum of U.S. defense capabilities.

U.S.-Japan-Republic of Korea Trilateral Cooperation

On March 31 of this year, President Obama held a trilateral meeting in Washington, DC with President Park and Prime Minister Abe in which the three leaders emphasized the importance of trilateral cooperation. After the meeting, President Obama said "we are bound together by treaty, by trade, and by the enduring bonds between our peoples." This trilateral cooperation has continued throughout the year. On May 30, Secretary of Defense Carter met in Singapore with his Japanese and ROK counterparts to discuss defense cooperation. Just last week, Secretary Kerry met with his Japanese and South Korean counterparts in New York. During that meeting, Secretary Kerry, Japanese Foreign Minister Kishida, and South Korean Foreign Minister Yun strongly condemned North Korea's September 9 nuclear test and its flagrant disregard for multiple United Nations Security Council Resolutions prohibiting the DPRK's ballistic missile and nuclear programs. Secretary Kerry and his counterparts also noted the positive role that the three countries can play to promote regional peace and stability and address global challenges. That emphasis is shared by diplomats and military leaders at all levels of our governments.

To further support and enhance trilateral ties, Secretary Kerry asked Deputy Secretary Blinken to lead an effort to institutionalize trilateral cooperation on regional security and global issues. Since April 2015, the Deputy Secretary has held five meetings with his counterparts from Japan and the Republic of Korea, the last of which occurred in July 2016 in Honolulu. We look forward to the next such meeting this fall. These meetings have guided our trilateral cooperation and have spurred lower-level engagement focused on specific functional issues.

Trilateral Cooperation on Regional Security

Our partnership with the Republic of Korea and Japan is strategic and focused on dealing with the threat that North Korea poses to the region and to the world. Special Representative for North Korea Policy Sung Kim meets regularly with his ROK and Japanese counterparts to coordinate all aspects of North Korea policy, and these trilateral consultations have deepened as the North Korean nuclear and missile threat has grown.

In June of this year, we conducted a joint missile warning exercise, called Pacific Dragon, to improve coordination in a number of areas, including the detection, tracking, and reporting of ballistic targets. Japan, the Republic of Korea, and the United States continue to exchange information on North Korea's capabilities. We are regularizing military-to-military engagements to strengthen ties among the three countries. Key diplomatic and defense officials from our three countries have worked together via the December 2014 Trilateral Information Sharing Arrangement to coordinate approaches on addressing the DPRK missile and nuclear threat. Immediately following North Korea's nuclear tests and missile launches this past year, State Department and Defense Department officials have also communicated with Japanese and Republic of Korea counterparts via trilateral phone and video conferences to coordinate our various responses.

We are also in lockstep with our Japanese and South Korean partners on finding ways to counter North Korea's proliferation activities. We are working together to ensure all countries understand and are able to implement fully their obligations under UN Security Council Resolution 2270, adopted in March 2016 in response to North Korea's January 2016 nuclear test. We've seen progress in key areas, such as disrupting the DPRK arms trade and de-flagging DPRK ships. We're focusing our efforts on cutting off sources of revenue for the regime's unlawful nuclear and ballistic weapons programs, including revenue generated through the coal trade and overseas by North Korean workers. We're also coordinating our efforts in multilateral forums, including the United Nations, the East Asia Summit, the International Civil Aviation Organization (ICAO), and the International Maritime Organization (IMO), to ensure that other countries join us in condemning North Korea's provocative actions and fully enforce UN sanctions against the regime.

Our three countries will continue to increase the costs on North Korea and target its revenue and reputation until it makes a strategic decision to return to serious talks on denuclearization and complies with its international obligations and commitments. We are doing our part to ensure the Kim regime knows its reckless provocations will only invite a stronger response and deepen its isolation from the international community. We have long made clear our willingness to take part in credible and authentic talks aimed at returning to the Six-Party Talks with the core goal of denuclearizing the DPRK. Unfortunately, the DPRK's litany of provocations demonstrates its rejection of the kind of dialogue and diplomacy that the Republic of Korea, Japan, and the United States seek.

Our strategic cooperation also goes beyond dealing with North Korea. For example, we all have a keen interest in upholding a rules-based order worldwide, one in which all countries, regardless of size, act according to shared norms and shared principles. All three of our countries are concerned about disputes in the South China Sea. The United States does not take a position with respect to which claimant has sovereignty over any of the naturally formed land features in the South China Sea, but we do take a strong position on the importance of all claimants resolving disputes peacefully and in accordance with international law, as reflected in the Law of the Sea Convention.

We have called upon both China and the Philippines to abide by the July Arbitral Tribunal decision and uphold international law. The United States will stand with allies and partners in upholding these fundamental interests, and the ongoing Deputy-level trilateral meetings give us a forum to discuss these issues with some of our closest allies in the region. We have also used our trilateral structure to cooperate on humanitarian assistance and disaster response to test our collective readiness on a range of natural disaster scenarios.

Trilateral Cooperation on Global Issues

While dealing with these regional security issues is critical, our trilateral engagement has evolved into a partnership that is global in scope. In today's interconnected world, epidemics, climate change, cyber attacks, and terrorist activities pay borders little heed, making coordination with allies and partners all the more important in responding to such threats.

Few countries have as much to contribute to upholding, advancing, and reforming the global system as our three countries – as vibrant democracies deeply invested in the principles and norms of that system, and as economic leaders for sustainable growth and game-changing innovation.

Allow me to give you a few examples of the results of our trilateral engagement on global issues. At the Women's Empowerment Forum today in Washington, DC, approximately 60 government, business, and civil society leaders, together with elected officials, from our three countries are meeting to discuss ways to bolster gender equality. The participants are focused on promoting women's political and economic participation in each of our three countries, as well as coordinating our gender-focused development programs throughout the world, with a particular interest in adolescent girls' education. This forum exemplifies the growth of our trilateral cooperation on global issues that matter to citizens in each of our countries.

We have also moved forward on cooperating on health issues that affect us all. Both the Republic of Korea and Japan have been active participants in the Global Health Security Agenda, the President's initiative to improve global capabilities to detect, prevent, and respond to infectious disease threats. As I mentioned above, Secretary Kerry met with counterparts from Japan and the Republic of Korea on the margins of the U.N. General Assembly earlier this month in New York. During the same week, Vice President Biden, along with the health ministers of our three countries met and made a commitment to work together on cancer research in connection with the Vice President's Cancer Moonshot initiative. Scientific leaders from our three countries also met in New York to discuss ongoing brain research projects. These trilateral initiatives on health will protect and benefit citizens in our three countries and across the world.

Our trilateral cooperation on global issues includes many other areas. This summer, our top Arctic officials discussed ways to foster scientific cooperation and our logging experts exchanged information and best practices on domestic logging laws, international law enforcement networking, and customs and borders enforcement. We have used our trilateral partnership to discuss ways to counter violent extremism in the Middle East, expand our cooperation on civil space exploration, work together in coping with emerging cyber threats, and coordinate our approaches to economic development.

As you can see, the breadth and scope of our trilateral cooperation is virtually unparalleled.

Fostering Improved Japan/Republic of Korea Relations

I also believe our trilateral engagement process has helped with the ongoing improvement in relations between the Republic of Korea and Japan. In December 2015, Japan and the Republic of Korea – under the leadership of Prime Minister Abe and President Park – reached an historic agreement to address the sensitive historical issue of "comfort women." We have applauded their courageous step, which, we believe, will contribute to healing and reconciliation, while creating new opportunities for greater bilateral and trilateral cooperation.

Conclusion

Mr. Chairman and Members of the Subcommittee, the Department of State is committed to enhancing trilateral cooperation among the United States, Japan, and the Republic of Korea to better confront shared regional and global challenges. We look forward to working with you and other Members of Congress to continue building this important trilateral relationship.

Thank you for inviting me to testify here today. I am pleased to answer any questions you may have.

Mr. SALMON. Thank you.

Mr. Russel, Mr. Sherman and I, and I think a couple others up here on the dais, were able to get a classified briefing last week on the North Korea nuclear proliferation issue. And I think we all left pretty unsettled with what has been going on.

One of the mitigating factors that is being touted or considered is THAAD. I know that, as I have talked to some of my South Korean counterparts about the commitment and deployment of THAAD, they have had some political hurdles to get through to ultimately get it accomplished. What is your prognosis for when we believe that THAAD will be able to be deployed in South Korea?

And the other sideline question of that or adjunct question to that would be, you know, the North Koreans are testing nuclear-delivered ballistic missiles. THAAD wouldn't really do anything to counter that. What are their capabilities to defend themselves if North Korea chose to actually deploy one with a nuclear warhead?

Mr. RUSSEL. Well, thank you, Mr. Chairman.

The alliance, the U.S. and the ROK, have made the decision to deploy the THAAD system purely as a defensive measure against the threat to the particular area where the U.S. military and ROK military are deployed. This is a defensive measure aimed not at China but at North Korea. It is a defense-based decision, not a political decision. And it is part of a layered system of defense that will augment the many military installations and systems currently in place.

I will have to defer to my colleagues in the Department of Defense for a more authoritative answer to the question about our missile defense overall. But deterrence and defense is a critical component of our overall strategy toward the DPRK. It is balanced by diplomacy on the one hand, of course, and serious pressure on the other.

But as North Korea accelerates its efforts to develop and perfect a missile technology that is capable of carrying a nuclear device as it accelerates its provocations, including the ballistic missiles that it has fired in violation of the Security Council resolution, including into the economic exclusive zone of Japan, our defensive systems are being upgraded. And a key part of that, of course, is the information sharing and the interoperability among the three allies: Japan, the Republic of Korea, and the United States.

Mr. SALMON. Do we believe that, I mean, optimistically, that that can be deployed by next year?

Mr. RUSSEL. I can't speak as the Assistant Secretary of State to the timeline. Perhaps our colleagues in the Defense Department and the Republic of Korea can. But, given the accelerating pace of North Korea's missile tests, we intend to deploy on an accelerated basis, I would say, as soon as possible.

Mr. SALMON. So, are all the political barriers that have heretofore been up in South Korea, are they—I mean, have they politically made the decision that they are firmly committed to this? And do you believe that pretty much—I mean, do you believe it is a done deal?

Mr. RUSSEL. Yes, I do, Mr. Chairman.

Mr. SALMON. Okay. That is really what I was looking for more than anything. And, I think optimistically, I have heard from some of our military folks that it can happen pretty quickly.

I am going to shift quickly to the sanctions that we have on North Korea right now, which haven't been incredibly effective, mostly due to China's lack of resolve in the implementation. Many experts propose that maybe the next step is to impose sanctions on specialized financial messaging services, which allow communications and transactions to banks that would fund North Korea's nuclear program.

This was done in the past with respect to Iran banking systems with great success, and I think it is past time for North Korea to be blocked from this kind of access as well. Adding to a long list of reasons in favor of this, analysts point to North Korea's recently having hacked specialized financial messaging services to steal upwards of $81 million from Bangladesh's central bank.

Is the administration sympathetic to the idea of pushing this kind of an idea forward? I am actually going to be introducing legislation tomorrow along these lines, and we would love to work with the administration to try to get it in place. Is this something you might be interested in helping us on?

Mr. RUSSEL. Thank you, Mr. Chairman. The SWIFT system, which is what I think you are referring to——

Mr. SALMON. Right.

Mr. RUSSEL [continuing]. Is not a U.S. system and therefore not under our direct control. I believe it is an EU system housed in Brussels. We are in discussions with our partners, including the EU, about tightening the application of sanctions and pressure, including and particularly to deny North Korea access to the international banking infrastructure that it has abused and manipulated in furtherance of its illicit programs.

I think that our hope is that we will, in fact, ultimately be able to reach an agreement that would further restrict North Korea's access. At the same time, the U.S. Government, and in particular the Department of the Treasury and OFAC, looks at North Korean banks, North Korean banking activities with a view to shutting down anything that might contribute to the illicit programs or otherwise violate the Security Council resolutions or our own laws.

Mr. SALMON. I think that we are going to have to step outside the paradigms that we have had in the past and try to figure out newer and more improved ways of putting the pressure on North Korea. I think most people realize that China poses a lot more leverage over North Korea than anybody else combined. But, with their reticence to really step up the pressure on North Korea, we are going to have to get, I think, more creative in finding other ways that we can limit their abilities.

My last question is, what are the chances that the Park government negotiates with a military information-sharing agreement with Japan?

Mr. RUSSEL. Well, Mr. Chairman, there is now a trilateral information security agreement, which dates back 1½ or 2 years. There are other steps and legal agreements that could be entered into by the two governments. This is something that, of course, we look forward to.

I can't speak for either of the two governments, but there has been a steady increase in practical cooperation and a willingness between the two governments and between the two militaries that is driven by clear-eyed recognition of the accelerating DPRK missile and nuclear threat. And I think that the logic of that threat is persuasively in favor of an additional agreement between the two militaries.

Mr. SALMON. It is my understanding that the General Security of Military Information Agreement is something that the administration has been very supportive of between Japan and South Korea. And let me just express our support here for accomplishing that as well, and anything that we can do to be helpful.

But, I think, like you just said, necessity is always the mother of invention. And, with what is going on with the expanded tests from North Korea, I think that it is going to push them to work more closely—all of us to work more closely together to deal with this great threat. But I thank the gentleman for his comments and I recognize Mr. Sherman for any questions he might have.

Mr. SHERMAN. Back in 2008, I believe it was, we took North Korea off the State Sponsors of Terrorism list. Since then, I can't say their behavior has improved. As a legal matter, the question is, do they still engage in terrorism? And I would point out that, at a minimum, we have got to focus on their kidnappings.

They kidnapped some to make movies. They kidnapped other innocent civilians to teach their spies etiquette. These kidnappings may have occurred decades ago, but they are still holding the kidnapped victims or their bodies. That is, of course, a continuing act of terrorism. Terrorism is not just dated on the date when you kidnap somebody; it continues until they are released.

Given the fact that they are still engaged in terrorism in that and other ways, given the fact that their nuclear behavior has hardly been modified, why isn't North Korea on the State Sponsor of Terrorism? You still have got a few months to get it done.

Mr. RUSSEL. The requirements under the legislation for listing or relisting a country, North Korea, under the State Sponsor of Terrorism provisions are set out in statute, and that is not something that we can change.

Mr. SHERMAN. I think the statute authorizes you or virtually directs you to list them as a state sponsor of terror.

Mr. RUSSEL. We look regularly for evidence that would warrant, that would justify placing the DPRK on that list.

Mr. SHERMAN. Kidnapping civilians and continuing to hold them, not to mention shelling South Korean territory. These are recent actions of the North Korean Government. Is there some provision that I am misreading in the legislation?

Mr. RUSSEL. Well, I can provide you, after double-checking exact language, with the——

Mr. SHERMAN. So you think that—would the administration support a legislative fix here simply designating North Korea as a state sponsor of terrorism? Would you oppose that?

Mr. RUSSEL. What we would do is to list North Korea under that provision if and when we had adequate evidence. Now, the——

Mr. SHERMAN. But, if we change the provision, then you don't have to do all that work.

Mr. RUSSEL. The kidnapping of Japanese citizens, of South Korean citizens, and the unwarranted detention of American citizens, all serious and unresolved problems, are high priorities for the administration.

Mr. SHERMAN. I am sure they are high priorities, but—we don't have enough time to deal with the statute. But it is very clear. You took—they have as much a right to be on that list as they did 10 years ago. But let me move on.

We have urged countries to give up their nuclear programs. Qadhafi and Saddam Hussein did. They are both dead. We might be able to get North Korea to give up its entire nuclear program, but only if we were able to exert regime-threatening pressure on the regime. And China is absolutely opposed to the regime buckling or coming close to buckling.

So we might consider a lesser objective, and that objective would be that we limit—that we freeze their nuclear program and freeze their missile test. That would be freezing them at a level that we found utterly unacceptable 10 and 15 years ago, but it is a lot better than not freezing it.

Secretary Kerry recently talked of a nonaggression pact and other concessions to the North Koreans. What does North Korea want? What pressure can we put on China in order to get not a non-nuclear North Korea—I don't think you can achieve that—but a frozen program?

Mr. RUSSEL. We believe, Mr. Sherman, that freezing North Korea's missile and nuclear program is a necessary first step in a longer process that leads to a rollback of their program and ultimately dismantlement of their program.

We agree that giving up the nuclear program is the last thing on Earth that North Korea's leader wants to do, and we are using robust and incremental application of sanctions to make that effectively the last thing that he can do. Part of that is to work with China to encourage the Chinese to use more of the very substantial leverage that we have. We have seen some progress on that foot.

Mr. SHERMAN. I want to try to sneak in one more question. Japan and South Korea both claim the islets known as the Liancourt Rocks. We have applauded the Philippines for going to UNCLOS with their dispute with China. We basically have said that the ruling of UNCLOS is final or binding there. What have we done to get Japan and South Korea to submit to UNCLOS or other international formal and binding adjudication of this dispute?

Mr. RUSSEL. Because UNCLOS doesn't address the issue of the underlying sovereignty claims anywhere, in the Liancourt Rocks or in the South China Sea, it is not a remedy to the dispute between the Republic of Korea and Japan over those——

Mr. SHERMAN. Well, there are other international tribunals that could be granted jurisdiction.

Mr. RUSSEL. Right. Both parties would have to agree to bring——

Mr. SHERMAN. Are we pushing them to agree?

Mr. RUSSEL. We are pushing them to pursue a peaceful process for resolving their differences. Whether it's a legal mechanism or a diplomatic mechanism is entirely up to them.

Mr. SHERMAN. We should clearly support whichever one is willing to submit to a legitimate adjudication, binding adjudication. Otherwise, they will just continue to disagree and it will continue to fester.

I will yield back.

Mr. SALMON. Thank you.

Mr. Rohrabacher.

Oh, I am sorry, Mr. Brooks. Apologies.

Mr. BROOKS. That is all right. I understand. I am way down here on the end.

Mr. Russel, I am not sure if you are familiar with some of America's financial situation advice we are getting. But I would note for the record that year after year now the Congressional Budget Office has warned Washington, Congress, White House, that our current financial spending habits are unsustainable. ''Unsustainable'' is their word.

Similarly, the comptroller general of the United States of America has in writing warned us that our spending habits are unsustainable, both of which suggest to me that, unless we change our ways, we are going to suffer a debilitating insolvency and bankruptcy of the United States of America.

In accord with that, way back in 2010 and 2011, the chairman of the Joint Chiefs of Staff, Admiral Mike Mullen, came before the United States Congress, House Armed Services Committee and testified twice that the greatest national security threat America faced was our deficit and accumulated debt.

With that as a backdrop, in my judgment, we need to try to find ways we can either be more efficient or where we can reduce our defense spending in different parts of the planet so that our core ability to defend the United States of America remains viable. If we go into insolvency and bankruptcy, we would not have that ability to defend our country.

So, with all that having been said, I note that we probably spend somewhere in the neighborhood of $7 billion, $8 billion, $9 billion defending Japan and South Korea, a substantial sum of money. Similarly, we spend a substantial sum of money—I am not sure the exact amount—concerning the South China Sea and disputes related to that. I think it is clear that there is still remnants of a schism between Japan and South Korea going back to World War II.

And my question is, if the United States were to reduce its involvement in the Western Pacific or Southeastern Asia because of these financial constraints being imposed on us, do you think that might force Japan and South Korea to work more closely together and to better defend not only their homelands but also that region of the world inasmuch as if we reduce our presence, they are forced to increase their presence or face increased unsatisfactory risk? What is your judgment in that vein?

Mr. RUSSEL. Well, thank you, Congressman Brooks.

Nature abhors a vacuum, and I think the same thing applies in geopolitics. Significant reduction of American presence, resolve, or necessary spending for defense, I think, would have a very destructive impact on both regional stability and the national interests of the United States. The Asia-Pacific region is the driver of economic growth. That rests on a foundation of stability that the U.S. has——

Mr. BROOKS. Well, I appreciate this insight you are sharing, but that is not answering my question. My question was, would that tend to force South Korea and Japan to start taking over a greater share of the burden of their own countries, the cost of defending their own countries, and perhaps taking a greater role in Southeast Asia and the Western Pacific?

Mr. RUSSEL. I think that that reduction on the part of U.S. spending and presence would open the door, frankly, to China to assert itself more vigorously. I think that——

Mr. BROOKS. Are you saying then that, in your judgment, Japan and South Korea would acquiesce to whatever China wanted, that they would not rise up and defend their interests?

Mr. RUSSEL. No. I think it would shake their confidence, however, in U.S. leadership and badly undermine both our deterrence and the credibility of American resolve.

Mr. BROOKS. Okay. You still haven't gotten to my question. My question is, would it force South Korea and Japan, in your judgment, to increase their spending? Yes or no?

Mr. RUSSEL. Right now, Japan spends in the neighborhood of $50 billion a year, plus a very significant amount in host nation support that allows us at a discount to——

Mr. BROOKS. I asked for a yes or no. Do you think it would force Japan and South Korea to spend more on national defense if they were not so able to rely on the United States of America to defend their homelands for them?

Mr. RUSSEL. It might have that effect, but that would be offset by the phenomenal consequences.

Mr. BROOKS. I didn't ask for the offset. I understand what the offsets are.

Same situation with respect to the South China Sea. If the United States were to reduce its presence there, would that tend to force Japan, South Korea, Taiwan, Vietnam, the Philippines, and Malaysia, even Brunei, to spend more on their national security needs and be more self-sufficient as opposed to their current reliance on the forces of the United States of America and the tax dollars of struggling Americans?

Mr. RUSSEL. I believe that a withdrawal of the U.S. presence from the South China Sea would result in a tactical accommodation by the countries of Southeast Asia with China.

Mr. BROOKS. Would that be good or bad if they started working more closely with Mainland China?

Mr. RUSSEL. It would not serve the U.S. national interest.

Mr. BROOKS. Why not?

Mr. RUSSEL. Because the Chinese strategy for the relationship of Asia would, in that circumstance, badly weaken America's ability to exercise our rights, everything from freedom of navigation to lawful commerce. It would contribute to the emergency of——

Mr. BROOKS. Well, let me interject. How would that interfere with our ability to ship goods back and forth between America and South Korea or Japan and the Philippines? We don't have to go through the South China Sea to get to any of those nations. Aren't those shipping lanes predominantly used by those Southeastern

19

and Western Pacific rim countries, not the United States of America, particularly with respect to, say, shipments of oil?

Mr. RUSSEL. Well, shipments of oil, certainly, may originate, or natural gas, may originate from the United States, but they don't come to the United States. Something on the order of $5 trillion of global trade——

Mr. BROOKS. Well, I was thinking more of Middle Eastern oil being shipped to Japan, South Korea, and the other Western Pacific rim countries.

Mr. RUSSEL. There is some of that, but globally, Congressman. But, particularly in an area of such economic importance to the United States, our ability to ensure both for ourselves and for others the unimpeded right to navigate, to conduct lawful commerce is at the heart of our economic interests as well as our national security interests.

Mr. BROOKS. Mr. Chairman, if I could just have one last question. Are you saying that the United States should continue to spend all this money we don't have, we have to borrow to get, we can't afford to pay back, regardless of the consequences, and we should make no effort to force any of these other Asian nations to increase national defense spending that is in their own interest?

Mr. RUSSEL. Well, other countries will decide what is in their own interest. Our relationships with our partners is not one of force; it is one of cooperation and one of persuasion. And the benefits and the funding that we obtain directly from our five treaty allies and our other security partners in the Asia-Pacific region is of immense value to the American people and the American Government.

Mr. BROOKS. Thank you, Mr. Chairman, for your indulgence.

Mr. SALMON. Thank you.

Mr. Bera.

Mr. BERA. Thank you, Mr. Chairman.

And thank you, Mr. Russel, for, you know, being in front of this committee once again.

I am going to choose to take a different approach. As I think about the Asia-Pacific region, it is of immense strategic importance to the United States and our national interests. You know, as a region on the rise, as the fastest growing economic region, but one that also poses significant threats to us and North Korea, you know, we can't withdraw from the region. I think there would be disastrous consequences.

It is also a region where the countries in that area are watching what our commitment to the Asia-Pacific region are and whether we will stand by those commitments. That is why, whether you support the TPP or are against the TPP, these are countries that we are going to have to trade with, and these are countries that we have significant economic interests in.

If you support engagement in the South China Sea or don't support engagement in the South China Sea, we are not talking about what is going to happen today. We are talking about setting the stage for what may happen a decade from now or two decades from now.

When you look at the relationship between United States, Japan, and Korea, you know, these are some of our deepest relationships and deepest allies, countries that have like values, countries that are democratic countries, countries that we have deep economic relations with. We have to stand by those allies and our commitments there.

Having visited our troops in Korea, you know, having gone through the DMZ, watching the complexity of how you approach North Korea, that is a major threat to us and that is a major threat to stability in the region. And, the stronger our ties with Korea and Japan, as well as the surrounding countries in Southeast Asia along with the burgeoning relationship with India, it does give us the opportunity to leverage what role China wants to take in the 21st century.

Certainly they are moving in a more autocratic confrontative direction, but it is not a given that we can't change that trajectory, and it is not a given that it is not in China's interest not to change that trajectory. In fact, you know, through economic engagement with our partners there, I think we can help China become a more responsible player in the 21st century.

And it is not lost on all of us that it is going to be very difficult to change North Korea's behavior, and there is no way to do that without Chinese cooperation and Chinese partnership and leadership in changing North Korea's behavior. The last thing we want to do is squander these opportunities today and end up in a kinetic war, or worse, a decade or two from now, because the cost of that would be much greater than the investments that we are making today.

You know, just in terms of—a few questions. If we look 2 years ago, 3 years ago, the relationship between Japan and Korea was not necessarily at its high point. We have seen Japan and Prime Minister Abe make some overtures, and it does seem like the relationship is at a much stronger place right now. I would be curious about your sense of where that relationship is, Mr. Russel.

Mr. RUSSEL. Well, thank you very much, Congressman Bera.

First, let me say, I fully agree with everything that you said. Secondly, I would like to say, lest I leave anyone with the impression that our strategy is in any way anti-China, that both our trilateral cooperation with Japan and Korea and our overall rebalance aims for a constructive, cooperative relationship with China. We do not seek to contain China. We probably couldn't if we tried. China couldn't expel us from the Pacific region. So finding constructive ways to cooperate and to manage our differences is and has been the top priority for the Obama administration. I think we have a good record there.

Similarly, both President Park and Prime Minister Abe have made great strides in establishing more constructive relationships with Beijing. In the case of South Korea, the extraordinary decision by President Xi to visit South Korea more than a year ago without ever having had any contact at all with the North Korean leader speaks volumes for the shift in the dynamics and the geostrategic alignment.

Prime Minister Abe had his senior staff negotiate, last year, a four-point agreement with China that established some principles for their bilateral relationship. He has assiduously made efforts to build a better relationship, better lines of communication, and find

21

ways to deal with their bilateral disputes in a constructive, peaceful, and lawful manner.

The Chinese, I would say, have been hot and cold. Sometimes things have looked like they were improving or there had been a standoff. The fact is, however, that Prime Minister Abe and President Xi Jinping have met in some fashion several times in the last year. I believe that there have been and will be meetings not only at the Foreign Minister level but also with the Chinese Prime Minister.

So I think it is fair to say that the trend line is positive, notwithstanding some very significant territorial and other disputes in the East China Sea.

Mr. BERA. Great. Thank you.

I will yield back.

Mr. SALMON. Thank you.

Mr. Rohrabacher.

Mr. ROHRABACHER. Thank you very much for being with us today.

And thank you, Mr. Chairman, for this hearing. This is a very important discussion.

Let me ask you just a few things about the nature of North Korea. Does North Korea have major universities for engineering and electronics and nuclear physics and things such as this?

Mr. RUSSEL. North Korea has certainly a major university, Kim Il-sung University, that has within it a variety of technical disciplines, and they may well have other programs.

Mr. ROHRABACHER. I guess what I am going to do, have they had the capacity within North Korea in order to develop this nuclear program that they have, or is it dependent on help from China?

Mr. RUSSEL. Well, I think that the opinion of most analysts is that the North Korean nuclear and missile program is largely based on technology know-how and material, either bought, stolen, or otherwise obtained from a variety of sources, including China—

——

Mr. ROHRABACHER. All right.

Mr. RUSSEL [continuing]. Combined with a great deal of resourcefulness and technical skill on the part of the North Koreans.

Mr. ROHRABACHER. Right. So we do recognize that this nutcase regime up in North Korea is not capable of actually building the missiles and the rockets and the nuclear bombs that they seem to be developing. And we also acknowledge that China has played some role in that, but we don't know how much of a role.

Is it adequate to say, if China really wanted to say, ''You will not be able to produce these nuclear weapons or these rockets,'' is it accurate to say that then the North Koreans would not be able to accomplish that goal?

Mr. RUSSEL. I don't know that we could say that with certainty, Congressman Rohrabacher, in part because the missile technology that North Korea has obtained over the years from Russia, for example, or the nuclear technology that it has obtained, whatever the source, it now forms a platform on which North Korean engineers continue to innovate and to moderate. So I don't think we can get them back to zero merely by choking off cooperation.

However, we have made great strides—and I believe that the Chinese themselves are now quite motivated—to try to prevent any additional nuclear technology or material from making its way into North Korea in support of their program.

Mr. ROHRABACHER. Just a couple more questions about the nature of the regime. This supreme leader, is he actually—we heard reports that he has murdered long-time staffers or people who had actually been advisers to his father. He murdered them and threw them to dogs to be eaten? Did that actually happen?

Mr. RUSSEL. I can't speak to the veracity of the report about dogs, in part because we have no way of verifying——

Mr. ROHRABACHER. But we do know that he has murdered. So, what you are saying, we do know that he has murdered some of his—even his top echelon of people that had worked for his father.

Mr. RUSSEL. Well, one of his relatively early acts was to order the execution of his own uncle.

Mr. ROHRABACHER. Of his own uncle. So what we have got is a monster, and he has everybody calling him the supreme leader. And this is obviously a horror story for his people. But, frankly, it is a threat to the world as well, and especially to Japan and to Korea, which are democratic countries.

Let me just suggest, it is time that Korea and Japan make the maximum effort to overcome any difficulties between them. And we talked about the Rocks that they have a dispute over. I would suggest right now that Japan, who we need to move forward in a rearmament program in order to thwart these forces that are at play in that part of the world, that Japan just give up any type of demand or recognition of those Rocks to Korea as a sign of good faith. Then, it should proceed and become a major partner of the United States. Partner, not junior partner but equal partner, along with, hopefully, Korea, a democratic Korea, in providing stability, which we can no longer afford to provide for them.

And my colleague was absolutely right when he talked about keep going the way we are. We are not going to be able to protect anybody 10 years from now because we will be bankrupt. So it is time we start doing these responsibly and equal partnership with Japan and then Korea, in providing a security blanket for that part of the world rather than American naval personnel having to do that, is the formula that works.

And I would hope that today, this hearing that comes out of this, is understanding that China is playing a negative role instead of a positive role in Korea and that the Koreans are run by this maniac who could end up murdering not only his own people but, with nuclear weapons, millions of other people. And thus, we need to make—have a strong force, and that will only be possible in the years ahead with Japan and Korea playing a more important role.

Mr. RUSSEL. Well, Congressman, we have no better allies or partners than Japan and the Republic of Korea. We value greatly not only their defense budgets and their defense equipment purchases from the United States, but also the host nation support that they provide to our troops who they allow us to station there.

Mr. ROHRABACHER. Well, thank you very much.

Thank you, Mr. Chairman.

Mr. SALMON. Thank you.

Mr. Lowenthal.

Mr. LOWENTHAL. Thank you, Mr. Chairman. And I want to thank you, Mr. Chairman, for holding this hearing. And we have all heard, I think, of the importance of the U.S., South Korea, and Japan's trilateral relationship.

And I want to thank you, Secretary Russel, as well as Secretary Kerry and Deputy Secretary Blinken for their work, all of it to deepen and strengthen this relationship. We are all democracies. We have already talked about that. We have strong alliances.

The question I would like to know is, which we have touched on it a little bit. I kind of want to just kind of talk about some of the things that you have raised. You have talked about—besides our strong trilateral relationship with Japan and South Korea and the United States, I am interested in what you see in the trilateral efforts that are going on between China, Japan, and South Korea. What is your view on these? Where do they really stand? And how do they compare with our trilateral relationship between these countries?

Mr. RUSSEL. Thank you, Congressman Lowenthal.

There is a longstanding trilateral trade process among Japan, China, and South Korea that has been frozen for approximately the last 2 years and is now only gradually being unfrozen as the Japanese hosted recently a foreign ministerial and are planning—are in the process of hosting a trilateral meeting at the Prime Minister's level. The process is significantly behind its intended schedule in terms of reaching an agreement on a free trade arrangement among these three countries.

The view of the United States is to welcome this sort of flexible combination of what we call multilateral geometry, the notion that different groupings of countries can make common cause for constructive purposes, and we certainly would put free trade in that category.

These are three of our major economic partners. For them to harmonize, rationalize, and improve their systems, certainly to move closer to the high standards that we advocate for is a desirable outcome. It is not moving with a great deal of rapidity, but we have no qualms about the prospect of their making progress. There is no political dimension to it, as far as I know.

And, although we see some value in the ability of the three Foreign Ministers or the three leaders to talk and to interact, that is always going to be good. It bears no resemblance whatsoever to the extensive, in-depth coordination and cooperation that is the hallmark of America's trilateral cooperation, either with Japan and Korea or, for that matter, with Japan and Australia.

Mr. LOWENTHAL. Let's talk about those others. What do you see then—you just mentioned Australia also—where these trilateral relationships that we have now with the United States, Korea, and Japan, where is it going in the future? Are there opportunities to bring Australia into that relationship? And can we imagine a time when it would make sense to also bring India into that relationship?

Mr. RUSSEL. The short answer is yes. And, in fact, we do have not only bilateral discussions but trilateral discussions with India and Japan. There have at different points been discussions of moving from trilateral to quadrilateral.

Mr. LOWENTHAL. Quadrilateral.

Mr. RUSSEL. You know, the sky is the limit. As a practical matter, my own experience as a diplomat is that three is a pretty good number for sitting down and really thrashing out, with some candor and some depth, our policies. But the fact is that among the major democracies in the Asia Pacific, the countries that share values and goals, this kind of collective action is important. These are inclusive processes. They are not exclusive.

And the fact of the matter is that the world would be a better place if there were more right thinking democracies in the Asia Pacific with whom we could deal, or frankly, if there were other countries, including one-party systems like Vietnam, like China, who would be willing, on the basis of high standards and international law, to engage in a constructive and a collaborative effort.

There are times when we have, in fact, been able to make effective common cause not only with Japan and Korea but also with China. And Resolution 2270, the U.N. Security Council resolution adopted last year, that imposed landmark sanctions on the DPRK was, in fact, the result of that loose coordination among the four of us.

Mr. LOWENTHAL. Thank you.

Thank you, Mr. Chair. I yield back.

Mr. SALMON. Thank you.

Mr. Chabot.

Mr. CHABOT. Thank you, Mr. Chairman.

It is great to have you back, Mr. Russel. I have enjoyed working with you over the years. And let me begin by a country—and I say ''country'' intentionally—that we haven't talked about this morning, and that is Taiwan, which is an American ally that is affected greatly by what happens in the Korean Peninsula and in the South China Sea, yet it remains outside of the conversation at least thus far this afternoon. I am going to bring it into the conversation.

Shouldn't we include Taiwan in any discussion of the region's security architecture? You know, if we are talking South Korea, we are talking about Japan, shouldn't we really be talking about Taiwan? Isn't the relationship with all three of those countries of great importance to the United States?

Mr. RUSSEL. Well, thank you very much, Congressman. I am a big fan of Taiwan. Taiwan is a tremendous friend to the United States and a very important democracy in Asia Pacific, a great model for others, and a significant contributor to not only the economic well-being of the region but also the safety, security, the humanitarian relief. We admire and value Taiwan's contributions.

Our policy and our approach to Taiwan is rooted in our one-China policy as informed by the three communications in the Taiwan Relations Act. We look for, and I personally engage on a regular basis with, to create opportunities for serious consultation and cooperation with the national security representatives from Taiwan.

Number one, we see value in Taiwan's ability to participate in international affairs and particularly in international organizations for which statehood is not a prerequisite, because we think they have a lot to offer.

Mr. CHABOT. Let me cut in, if I could. I have only got—half my time is gone, and I want to ask some other countries as well as Taiwan.

So, respectfully, you know, I think the world disses Taiwan. I think they are left out of a lot of organizations they ought to be involved in, and it is because of bullying by the PRC, by the People's Republic of China, who still considers them a breakaway province, which is absurd. It is a de facto country, and they have been independent for a long time now, and I think will be some day. They really are now.

But, again, China has been a bully, and the world has let itself be bullied by China, including the United States in this, which I think is pretty embarrassing. There seems to be a renewed movement, and we have seen some of the folks here on Capitol Hill, that China—excuse me—that Taiwan should be allowed to be a member of the U.N., for example, that it is embarrassing.

And the Olympics that we just saw, which was really exciting for a lot of us in the U.S. The U.S. did great. Our athletes were wonderful. And a lot of the other athletes around the world, you know, were a great honor to their country. But poor Taiwan has to come in as Chinese Taipei. That is ridiculous. That is embarrassing. And the world ought not to insist on that type of disregard for this country.

The U.S.—you know, that is the world, but the U.S.—the President of Taiwan can't come to Washington, DC. The Vice President of Taiwan can't come to Washington, DC. The Defense Minister, the Foreign Minister—some years ago, Mark Chen, who became the Foreign Minister, I had met with him about a month earlier, and we were going to get together. But he had been made Foreign Affairs Minister—I had to drive to Baltimore to meet with him up in Baltimore, because we couldn't legally meet in the capital of the United States. That is ridiculous. It is outrageous, and it ought to be changed. So, any comment?

Mr. RUSSEL. We are bound by and as eight administrations have, faithful to our one-China policy. But I think Taiwan's security and Taiwan's democratic system, its economic autonomy, frankly, Congressman, are higher priorities for me, for us, than the issue of nomenclature.

We are able to talk to the Taiwanese. We are able to consult and support and to accord them the respect and the dignity that they deserve.

Mr. CHABOT. They don't give them enough dignity, the dignity that they deserve. I agree that, you know, we are—with Taiwan Relations Act and other things, that we work closely with them, and obviously, they are a very strong ally, but the world needs to wake up on this. And there are so many other issues that are probably on the front burner, and to some degree I think the world looks at this as a back-burner issue. I don't think it is a back-burner issue.

You know, you have got, what, 26 million people that freely and democratically elect their people and have a right to be on the world stage just like every other country. And to hell with the PRC on this. I think this bullying has to end, and we ought to be part of that. And I think the PRC depends on us a heck of a lot more than we depend on them, and I think we ought to start recognizing that. And thank you for your time.

Mr. SALMON. Mr. Russel, I have another question. It is more related to North Korea's nuclear program. But the amount of fissile material that they have and the fact that they have now detonated, what is it, five nuclear weapons over the last several years tells us that they have significant nuclear resources, and they are not afraid to show the world that they have it.

One of the big concerns that I have as they move toward actually putting together a workable nuclear weapon is the potential that they would have in selling that to another rogue state, such as Iran. So Iran's going to have a lot of money, and North Korea has nuclear—potentially, nuclear weapons. What kind of safeguards are in place to ensure that a transaction like that doesn't occur and that Iran gets a nuclear weapon through the back door from North Korea, or even more frightening, ISIS gets a nuclear weapon from North Korea or Pakistan gets a nuclear weapon from North Korea? What are your concerns about that and, you know, how can we effectively deal with those concerns?

Mr. RUSSEL. Well, thank you, Mr. Chairman. Look, four—you know, four consecutive administrations have grappled with the problem of North Korea's determination to develop a nuclear weapons program. And, particularly in the last 15 years, we have been increasingly focused on preventing or minimizing the risk of proliferation directly with the North Koreans in every diplomatic encounter dating back as long as I have been involved. We have made a very forceful warning of the risk and the consequences to the DPRK if they undertook to proliferate either technology, fissile material, let alone a nuclear device.

Secondly, our intelligence networks and those of our partners monitors intently to seek to detect any indication or telltale that the North Koreans were pursuing that. We do not have any evidence currently that North Korea is attempting to export technology or device, but we are not going to stop looking.

What we are able to do under the U.N. Security Council resolutions as a result of both the North Korea Sanctions Act and, importantly, the executive order implementing that, is to create very serious headwinds; that is, by cutting off North Korea's ability to move its ships, to fly its planes, to get visas, or to allow its officials or, frankly, its pseudobusiness people to transit major international airports or to be allowed to enter foreign countries.

In doing so, we have made it more difficult, not impossible, but much more difficult for the DPRK should they attempt to market nuclear material or technology. We are very attentive to this risk and have established and utilized a broad international network to try to ensure that the North Koreans are never successful, should they try.

Mr. SALMON. I would think that potential should be something that, as a trilateral relationship that we have, that it ought to be on the minds of all policymakers from all of our nations. Because, given the fact that North Korea, to say that they are in the economic doldrums would be probably the misquote of the century.

Their economy is in the tank, and the people are starving. And there are a lot of despots out there that would pay pretty top dollar for a nuclear weapon if they could get their hands on it.

So it seems like the motivation could be there, and I think it is something we need to be really vigilant on and watching together with our allies to make sure that a transaction like that doesn't occur, because the results would be cataclysmic.

Mr. RUSSEL. We entirely agree. And I think that as frustrated and unhappy as all of us are at North Korea's ability to continue to develop its missile and its nuclear programs, the scorecard of the administration shows very significant successes in terms of alliance, coordination, including specifically on proliferation; a vast improvement and cooperation by China, even though as President Obama said very clearly when he was in China, there is an awful lot more tightening that the Chinese need to do, sanctions.

And, similarly, through the international network, and that means in the Middle East, it means in Africa, it means in Eastern Europe, it means in Latin America as well, we have used both the tools of the executive order and the Security Council resolution to raise the hurdles to the DPRK, either to export technology or material or to obtain financing. And we have—there is more coming in terms of sanctions.

Mr. SALMON. I certainly hope I wasn't trying to cast aspersions on, you know, the administration's efforts to thwart this, because it is an age-old problem. It didn't just happen with the current administration. It's been something that past administrations, as you have aptly said, have grappled with.

I think we should always be constantly looking for more alternatives to tighten the screws to make sure that we do stop this proliferation. But I am not sure without a much more robustly incentived China to get this problem taken care of, that anybody can get their arms around it. I think China is the 100-pound gorilla. And, so far, I don't think they have even come close to doing responsibly what they could and should do.

And so I am not laying blame. If there is any real blame, I think it is on China's acquiescence—or reticence, excuse me, to, you know, tighten the screws a little bit tighter with North Korea.

With that, I am going to yield to the ranking member.

Mr. SHERMAN. I want to pick up on the comments of the gentleman from Ohio briefly and then of the chairman.

We at least ought to let the Taiwanese President refuel at BWI and explain to our friends in Beijing that the B stands for Baltimore, and that is the first. I realize that is a less significant change. It is odd for me to be arguing for the less significant change, but I hope you would move there.

But I want to move to this, because I have been very concerned about the possible sale of a weapon or fissile material from North Korea to Iran. I had a chance—and this is a rare, very rare opportunity for me. I spent an hour with the President in the Oval Office on this a year ago—almost a year ago, and he gave answers consistent to yours on the fact that we have stopped North Korean ships. And, as you pointed out, there are sanctions on North Korean planes. So if this deal goes down, it will not be a North Korean ship, it will not be a North Korean plane. It will be an Iranian plane.

And we just licensed the sale to Iran of planes that could easily go nonstop from Tehran to Pyongyang with, say, about $1.7 billion of currency, euros, and Swiss franks loaded on planes wrapped in cellophane, which they just happen to have.

I don't think the sale will be to a terrorist group, because I don't think North Korea would part with this for just a few $100 million. And thank God there is no terrorist group that can really get its hands on $1 billion. So we are talking about North Iran—I mean, get its hands on $1 billion and continue to operate. Iran or a state sponsor of terrorism can get its hands on $1 billion.

We saw in 2007, the Israelis destroyed a plutonium reactor in Syria. That was North Korean technology paid for by the Syrian, or more likely the Iranian Government, at a time when North Korea could not part with fissile material because they didn't have 12 nuclear weapons.

I respect the chairman for not casting aspersions on this administration, but this is the first administration where North Korea has had—or was about to have enough nuclear weapons to defend themselves from us and still have more that they could sell. And to compliment the administration, you have got them in a situation where they really need some money.

And there is also the North Korean-Iranian cooperation on missile technology. So we know they are talking. We know they are doing deals. We know one of them has money. We know another one needs money. We know one has a surplus or assumed surplus of fissile material. We know another one, Iran, would like to have an indigenous enrichment capacity, but I think would settle for a purchased nuclear weapon or two, given the fact that the two individuals who America hated most that didn't have nuclear weapons were Qadhafi and Saddam, and they are both dead.

There is a question in here, because I would like you to do something. There is only one way to stop this, really, and that is to make it clear to the Chinese that they cannot allow a nonstop plane between Iran and North Korea, because if it is heading toward North Korea, it could have currency on it. If it is heading the other way, it could have fissile material on it. If it stops in China, I think China will inspect it.

So what do we do to make it clear to China that if there is just one nonstop round trip plane, that the President of Taiwan will be giving an address to a joint session of Congress and, by God, stopping at Dulles Airport on their way to do it? What can we do to make it clear to China, one nonstop plane, one speech before Congress?

Mr. RUSSEL. Well, thank you, Congressman Sherman, for your very creative diplomatic proposal.

Mr. SHERMAN. Feel free to say or a 10 percent tax on all Chinese imports or a ban on all shoe imports or whatever—well, you can substitute whatever you want. But if you don't lay this down, China will just relax as they have. And, by the way, I brought this up with Chinese—with the chairman of their foreign policy committee, et cetera, and they don't care. They are not going to act unless you make them.

Mr. RUSSEL. Well, thank you, Congressman. You will understand, there are limits to how far I can go in an unclassified open session. But I will say that I do think that the Chinese, in fact, care. My experience is that the Chinese have a self-interest in mitigating the risk of DPRK——

Mr. SHERMAN. If I can interrupt. They also have a very strong self-interest in the survival of the Pyongyang regime. If that collapses, they get millions of refugees and they get an American army on their border, and we have not committed publicly and in a binding manner not to move north of 38 parallel, something we probably should be doing as part of our overall discussions.

So they have a very strong interest in the survival of this regime, and $1.7 billion worth of euros and Swiss franks wrapped in cellophane would go a long way toward assuring the survival of a regime. So China has interests on both sides.

Mr. RUSSEL. We are in regular discussion at multiple levels with the Chinese about the risk of North Korean proliferation. I think that my professional observation is that we currently have functional channels that allow us to flag both concerns and the potential for an action along the lines that you are describing where technology or money moves into or out of the DPRK with a reasonable expectation of Chinese cooperation.

Mr. SHERMAN. I won't ask for anything that you shouldn't disclose in open session. But, please, make it very explicit, no nonstop flights.

Mr. RUSSEL. Thank you.

Mr. SALMON. I thank the gentleman.

Mr. Lowenthal, do you have another question?

Mr. LOWENTHAL. Yeah. I am just going to follow up on what Mr. Sherman has talked about. And, you know, we talked about putting a lot of pressure on the Chinese, and I think the chairman talked about tightening the screws to the Chinese. Given that that is one approach, which we should be doing, I am not disagreeing with that, but I also want to follow up with what Mr. Sherman said about some of the reasons why it is too—that China fears a weakened North Korea, that there are reasons that China now has some concerns about refugees coming across into China if there was a weakened collapse, a militarized Korea with the United States on its border, as he pointed out.

Are there room for discussions around all of these issues?

Mr. RUSSEL. Yes, there are. And I think that one of the hallmark accomplishments of the Obama administration is building mechanisms that permit real dialogue between the U.S. and China at appropriately senior levels that allow for candid exploration of where our interests overlap or diverge.

One such conversation was held just 2 or so weeks ago, 3 weeks ago, in Hangzhou, China, between President Obama and President Xi Jinpin. And there, they discussed in considerable depth the challenge that we each face from North Korea and its science. The Chinese were able to put on the table very directly their concerns about some of our moves, defensive moves, to mitigate North Korean missile threats like the deployment of the THAAD battery.

Mr. LOWENTHAL. That is right.

Mr. RUSSEL. The President was able to point out that the United States will not compromise with our security or with the security of our allies; that if China has specific concerns, we are happy to explore mitigating moves, but we are not prepared to stand down on necessary defense measures.

Now, I think that the trend line overall is toward increased cooperation between the U.S. and China. I think that we share an interest in preventing North Korea from being accepted as a nuclear state, from continuing with a nuclear weapons and a missile program. The Chinese frequently say to us that they want to prevent war on the Korean Peninsula, they want to prevent chaos on the Korean Peninsula, and they want to prevent nuclearization; namely, North Korea's successful pursuit of its program.

Now, as you point out, they have other concerns as well. I think it is a mistake to presume that the Chinese are so focused on either the threat from refugees or the risk of a U.S. presence in a unified Korea that they will not act in concert with the United States or at least be cooperative with the United States and the Republic of Korea. We have—we each have somewhat different interests and perspectives, but there is a very significant degree of overlap, a very constructive and honest, candid set of ongoing conversations. And I hope that you will see, as one of the products of that, real headway in the discussions in New York between our permanent representatives over the next generation U.N. Security Council resolution imposing even more sanctions on the DPRK.

Mr. LOWENTHAL. I just want to say, I think that there is room for creative solutions here, and I encourage the going forward. I am not here to micromanage or say what they are, but, you know, as I pointed out when I first said, we can go down one road, and maybe it is an appropriate road to put pressure, but on the other hand, there are many other roads that also lead to a successful resolution that need to be also explored, and acceptance that some of the concerns that China has are real, need to be addressed, need not—and need to figure out together and probably with Korea— with Republic of Korea and also with Japan, some of these issues, because they will impact all.

Mr. RUSSEL. Definitely.

Mr. LOWENTHAL. Thank you. And I yield back.

Mr. SALMON. Thank you.

I think we have probably asked you everything that is on our minds, at least for the last hour. And we will look forward to the next opportunity we have. Mr. Russel, thank you so much for your great work and everything that you have done.

Mr. RUSSEL. If I may, Mr. Chairman, the only point that I would like to add is that the unity of purpose between the Congress and the executive branch and the bipartisan solidarity in facing both the threat posed by North Korea and in grasping the opportunity to present it through trilateral coordination with our two close democratic partners in Northeast Asia is, I believe, a source of tremendous strength for the United States, and it serves the Republic very well.

So, again, I want to thank you for the tremendous leadership that you have shown over the last 2 years. And it's been my honor to serve in my position while you were chairman of this sub-committee. Thank you.

Mr. SALMON. Thank you very much, Mr. Russel.

Without further ado, we will adjourn this subcommittee.

[Whereupon, at 4:19 p.m., the subcommittee was adjourned.]

APPENDIX

MATERIAL SUBMITTED FOR THE RECORD

34

SUBCOMMITTEE HEARING NOTICE
COMMITTEE ON FOREIGN AFFAIRS
U.S. HOUSE OF REPRESENTATIVES
WASHINGTON, DC 20515-6128

Subcommittee on Asia and the Pacific
Matt Salmon (R-AZ), Chairman

September 27, 2016

TO: MEMBERS OF THE COMMITTEE ON FOREIGN AFFAIRS

You are respectfully requested to attend an OPEN hearing of the Committee on Foreign Affairs, to be held by the Subcommittee on Asia and the Pacific in Room 2172 of the Rayburn House Office Building (and available live on the Committee website at http://www.ForeignAffairs.house.gov):

DATE: Tuesday, September 27, 2016

TIME: 2:00 p.m.

SUBJECT: The U.S.– Republic of Korea–Japan Trilateral Relationship: Promoting Mutual Interests in Asia

WITNESS: The Honorable Daniel R. Russel
Assistant Secretary
Bureau of East Asian and Pacific Affairs
U.S. Department of State

By Direction of the Chairman

The Committee on Foreign Affairs seeks to make its facilities accessible to persons with disabilities. If you are in need of special accommodations, please call 202/225-5021 at least four business days in advance of the event, whenever practicable. Questions with regard to special accommodations in general (including availability of Committee materials in alternative formats and assistive listening devices) may be directed to the Committee.

COMMITTEE ON FOREIGN AFFAIRS

MINUTES OF SUBCOMMITTEE ON _____ *Asia and the Pacific* _____ HEARING

Day___*Tuesday*___Date_____*9/27/16*_____Room_____*2172*_____

Starting Time _____*2:50pm*_____ Ending Time _____*4:18pm*_____

Recesses [____] (____to____) (____to____) (____to____) (____to____) (____to____) (____to____) .

Presiding Member(s)

Salmon

Check all of the following that apply:

Open Session ☑   Electronically Recorded (taped) ☐
Executive (closed) Session ☐   Stenographic Record ☐
Televised ☐

TITLE OF HEARING:

The U.S.– Republic of Korea–Japan Trilateral Relationship: Promoting Mutual Interests in Asia

SUBCOMMITTEE MEMBERS PRESENT:

Brooks, Rohrabacher, Chabot
Sherman, Gabbard, Bera, Lowenthal, Meng, Connolly

NON-SUBCOMMITTEE MEMBERS PRESENT: *(Mark with an * if they are not members of full committee.)*

HEARING WITNESSES: Same as meeting notice attached? Yes ☑ No ☐
(If "no", please list below and include title, agency, department, or organization.)

STATEMENTS FOR THE RECORD: *(List any statements submitted for the record.)*

TIME SCHEDULED TO RECONVENE _____
or
TIME ADJOURNED _____*4:18pm*_____

Subcommittee Staff Associate

www.ingramcontent.com/pod-product-compliance
Lightning Source LLC
Chambersburg PA
CBHW081802280526

45789CB00008B/2967